Henry Wadsworth Longfellow and His Portland Home

Built in 1785-1786, the Wadsworth-
Longfellow House, boyhood home
of Henry Wadsworth Longfellow,
served three generations of the fami
before opening as a museum in
1901. Its centennial restoration in
2000-2002 recreated architectural
and decorative elements documente
to the 1850s.

Henry Wadsworth Longfellow and His Portland Home

Joyce Butler

Richard D'Abate

Laura Fecych Sprague

MAINE HISTORICAL SOCIETY • 2004

THE WADSWORTH-LONGFELLOW HOUSE is owned and cared for by the Maine Historical Society, founded in 1822, the third-oldest historical organization in the United States. The Society's mission is to promote the understanding and enjoyment of Maine history, which it does through its museum, library, online sites, publications, and educational programs. The Society collects, preserves, and exhibits important historical resources and treasures; it facilitates research into family, local, regional, and national history; and it provides learning opportunities that engage the public and make history accessible and meaningful.

The publication of this guide celebrates the restoration of the Wadsworth-Longfellow House, 2000-2002, which was made possible by the gifts of many generous individuals, foundations, and government agencies. Additional funding for this book was contributed by Furthermore of the J. M. Kaplan Fund, the P. W. Sprague Memorial Foundation, and Elsie Viles.

© Maine Historical Society 2004
ISBN 0-915592-35-5, SOFTCOVER
ISBN 0-915592-36-3, HARDCOVER

Designed by Scott Vile of The Ascensius Press.
Printed by PenMor Lithographers, Lewiston, Maine.

J. David Bohl took new architectural photographs of the Wadsworth-Longfellow House and its fine and decorative arts collections. Objects illustrated are from the collections of the Maine Historical Society, unless noted below.

Front cover: The earliest known photograph of the Wadsworth-Longfellow House was presented to Alexander Longfellow, the poet's brother, in November 1867. Courtesy, National Park Service, Longfellow National Historic Site.

Historic parlor photograph by Jackson and Kinney, page 8, courtesy, Maine Historic Preservation Commission.

Watercolor drawing by Anna M. Bucknam, page 13, jointly owned by Maine Historical Society and Maine State Museum.

Historic photograph by Mary King Longfellow, page 18, courtesy, the Talbot Family.

Floor plan drawn by Scott Benson, page 22, *Agreeable Situations* archive, courtesy, The Brick Store Museum.

Historic photograph of Anne Pierce, page 29, courtesy, National Park Service, Longfellow National Historic Site.

Historic dining room photograph attributed to Edward Lamson, page 30, courtesy, Maine Historic Preservation Commission.

Portland artist Charles Octavius Cole painted this compelling portrait of Henry Wadsworth Longfellow in 1842. It depicts the poet during his rising career and tenure at Harvard College. According to tradition, Longfellow saw it in the artist's studio and asked Cole to leave it unfinished. It is said to have been the poet's favorite portrait of himself.

Henry Wadsworth Longfellow:
A Literary Man

Richard D'Abate

Henry Wadsworth Longfellow was a commanding figure in the cultural life of nineteenth-century America. Born in Portland, Maine, in 1807, he became a national literary figure by the 1850s, and a world-famous personality by the time of his death in 1882. He was a traveler, a linguist, and a romantic who identified with the great traditions of European literature and thought. At the same time, he was rooted in American life and history, which charged his imagination with untried themes and made him ambitious for success.

Longfellow published his first poem in 1820, at the age of thirteen, in the *Portland Gazette*. It was a precocious sign of a precocious literary calling. By the time he graduated from Bowdoin College in Brunswick, Maine, five years later, his sense of purpose was complete. His father Stephen, concerned about his son's future, argued in favor of taking up the law. Longfellow was willing to acquiesce but he wrote: "I most eagerly aspire after future eminence in literature, my whole soul burns most ardently after it, . . . if I can ever rise in the world, it must be by the exercise of my talents in the wide field of literature."[1] Stephen, a trustee of Bowdoin, was not deaf to his son's enthusiasm and may have been instrumental in securing for him a professorship at the college in modern European languages—then a relatively new academic field. To prepare, Longfellow would first travel and study abroad.

His trip began in 1826 and lasted three years. It was the first of a number in his lifetime that would take him throughout Europe and Scandinavia, lead to the acquisition of nearly seven languages, and introduce him to both the classical literatures and the living authors of many countries. From this first trip also came his first youthful book and some indication of his literary temperament. It was a meditative travelogue called *Outre Mer: A Pilgrimage Beyond the Sea* (1835). We can see at once from *Outre Mer* that Longfellow is filtering his experience through the work of other writers—in this case Washington Irving's travel sketches and Lord Byron's *Childe Harold's Pilgrimage*. Later in his career he would be accused by Edgar Allan Poe of plagiarizing, but it is clear that Longfellow's use of literary models came from a deep sense of his participation in a universal fellowship of art: to borrow and imitate was to enrich and amplify his own vision. He was, we might say, a completely literary man: imaginatively engaged with works of literary genius; generous to other writers, whom he translated and published regularly; and in love with the act of writing and the power of language. "Study of languages, . . ." he wrote to his family on that first trip to Europe, "is like being born again."[2]

Longfellow began teaching French, Spanish, and Italian at Bowdoin in 1829. He soon married Mary Potter of Portland, began to write critical essays, and published six foreign language textbooks. It was enough to earn him the Smith Professorship of Modern Languages at Harvard College, which he accepted in 1834, beginning a long association with the city of Cambridge, Massachusetts. Longfellow would, however, always retain his ties to family and home in Maine.

To improve his language skills before taking on the new position, he and his wife and two friends left for Europe in 1835. It was to be a crucial turning point. On this trip life's lessons fell harder on Longfellow than they had ever done before. His young wife, Mary, died of a complicated miscarriage. After burying her, he continued his journey in a near suicidal depression, hoping that travel might dispel his cares. Solace did eventually come, but with it a new form of anguish. A chance meeting in the Swiss Alps brought Longfellow together with the wealthy Appleton family of Boston. It was then he met and fell in love with their daughter, the stylish and beautiful Frances (Fanny). Fanny Appleton was the great love of Longfellow's life, but she did not return that love, and would not for the next seven years.

Both bereaved and spurned, Longfellow returned to Cambridge to take up his teaching post. It was December 1836, and he was almost thirty years of age. We may say that he had become mature, or that he had finally glimpsed the real depths of human experience, but however we explain it, it is clear that the true beginning of Longfellow's creative life dates from this moment. In the next fifteen years he would write all the works on which his extraordinary and nearly instantaneous fame came to rest. *Hyperion*, an autobiographical *roman a clef*, appeared in 1839. The poem collections *Voices in the Night* (1839) and *Ballads and Poems* (1841) were received enthusiastically by an international audience. The great American novelist, Nathaniel Hawthorne, who had been a Bowdoin class-

H W Longfellow of Cambridge
Boston Dec 7 1841.

Longfellow's dashing full-length silhouette was cut by Auguste Edouart, a well-known profilist. It is inscribed "H W Longfellow of Cambridge / Boston Dec 7 1841."

mate of Longfellow's and would eventually become his life-long friend, wrote: "I read your poems over and over . . . nothing equal to some of them was ever written in this world." There followed *Poems on Slavery* (1844), the anthology *The Poets and Poetry of Europe* (1845), *Evangeline* (1847), the novel *Kavanagh* (1849), *The Song of Hiawatha* (1855), *The Courtship of Miles Standish* (1858), and *Tales of a Wayside Inn* (1863).

Clever marketing, often initiated by the poet himself, expanded the audience for all these works, until Longfellow had become one of the best-selling and most widely-read authors in the world. His early fame and persistent wooing finally led Fanny to relent, and they were married in 1843. Craigie House, the Cambridge residence most closely associated with the mature Longfellow, was a wedding gift from Fanny's father. He and Fanny raised their six children here and formed the warm family circle that, through its reflection in many poems, became a kind of national symbol for domestic love, the innocence of childhood, and the pleasure of material comfort. It was here, too, that Longfellow's famous circle of friends and acquaintances came—Emerson, Hawthorne, Oliver Wendell Holmes, Charles Sumner, Charles Eliot Norton, James Russell Lowell—as well as thousands of unknown visitors, for whom the house was a kind of shrine. By 1854 Longfellow was able to resign his teaching post at Harvard; he had become, at age forty-seven, one of America's first, self-sustaining authors.

The last and somewhat diminished stage of Longfellow's career began in 1861 with the tragic death of his wife Fanny. In the midst of melting sealing wax, she set fire to her own gauzy clothing and was enveloped in flames. She died the next day. In his futile efforts to put the fire out, Longfellow burned his hands and face, and it was to hide his facial scars that he eventually grew the beard that gave him the sage, avuncular look repro-

Henry Longfellow sent this engraving of Evangeline by James Faed to his sister, Anne Longfellow Pierce, in 1855. It was one of two prints of Longfellow's tragic heroine to decorate the parlor of the Portland house.

duced in so many later paintings and photographs, such as the famous Julia Margaret Cameron image. The death of his wife, perhaps amplified by the horrors of the Civil War, produced a deep and debilitating melancholy in Longfellow that would last until his death. His production of original poems slacked considerably. The greatest part of his energy went into the translation of Dante's *Divine Comedy*, one of the great monuments of world literature, as well as a prolonged meditation on the spiritual power of love to overcome death. It was published in 1867. Though he continued to write fine verse, Longfellow's most famous work was done. The fame itself, however, continued to grow. Honors of every kind were bestowed on him in Europe and America; he was received by heads of state, including Queen Victoria, who read and appreciated his work; he became acquainted with Dickens, Tennyson, Ruskin, Gladstone, Whitman, and even Oscar Wilde. His seventieth birthday, in 1877, became a national celebration. His death, five years later, produced national mourning.

What was it about Longfellow's writings that so moved people? It is important that modern readers dip back into Longfellow to see for themselves, but a few points are clear. His lyric poetry was supple, melodic, lucid, and filled with a curious mixture of moody tenderness and moral intensity. He borrowed Christian sentiment, but left the theological machinery behind.

This helped strike a new, secular, but still reverent note. One can imagine the thrill of reading these lines from *A Psalm of Life* for the first time in 1839:

> *Trust no Future, howe'er pleasant!*
> *Let the dead Past bury its dead!*
> *Act, – act in the living Present!*
> *Heart within, and God o'erhead!*[3]

And then there are his epic poems of the American past, such as *Evangeline*, *Hiawatha* and *The Courtship of Miles Standish*. It is useful to recall that one of Longfellow's favorite metaphors is the backward glance. People in the present look back into their distant pasts and make a discovery. What had once been history—political, conflicted, sad, and bloody—could now be seen as imaginative myth: ordered, noble, and a source of strength. Longfellow wrote for a young nation ready to make this backward glance. The Indian, displaced or all but extinct; the too rigid Puritans; the French Acadians, driven into exile by the English—all had, seemingly, sacrificed their identities on America's vast stage. In return they would become our originating legends. It was Longfellow's genius and unique opportunity to supply his country with its mythic past, and for this he was loved.

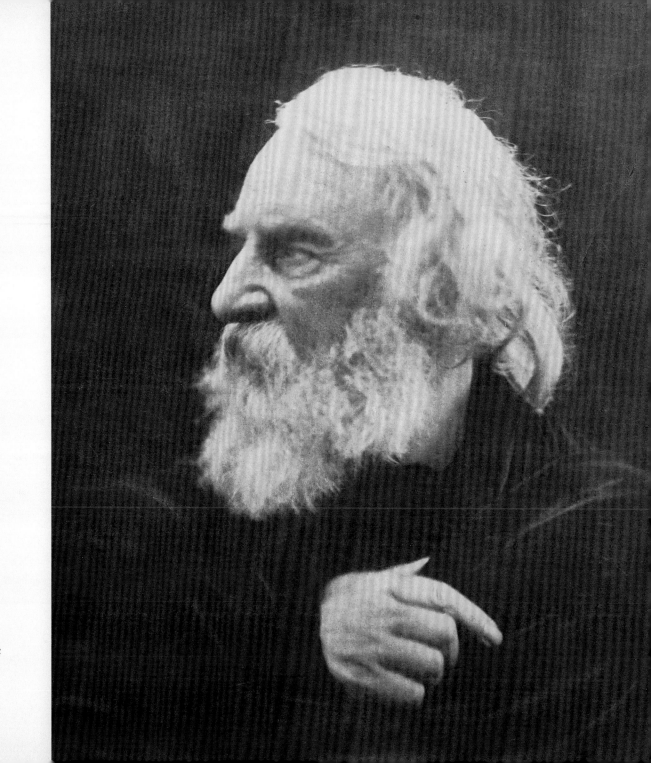

Julia Margaret Cameron photographed Longfellow during his visit to London in 1868. It is one of the best-known images of the poet.

Henry Wadsworth Longfellow appears in this oil portrait, attributed to Thomas Badger, dressed in his scholar's gown. He was a young professor at Bowdoin College when this portrait was painted in Portland around 1832. Fanny Appleton Longfellow, seeing it in the parlor for the first time, remarked how "like" it was.

Henry Wadsworth Longfellow and His Family

JOYCE BUTLER

Henry Wadsworth Longfellow's ancestry is recorded in his name. The Wadsworth and Longfellow families were representative of New England's modest, old-stock, cultural elite. In the early Republic they became part of the rising middle class. His grandfathers and father were patriots and public servants whose participation in the founding of a new nation imbued the entire family with a conscious sense of history. In religious matters Henry's parents—his mother in particular—avoided stern sectarianism in favor of more liberal and progressive spiritual ideals. The family read avidly, drew, painted, played music, and wrote voluminously, often with flair and humor. It was in this family, in the house on Congress Street, in Portland, Maine, that Henry Wadsworth Longfellow was nurtured and educated.

The Wadsworths

In 1784 Peleg and Elizabeth Bartlett Wadsworth, the poet's maternal grandparents, arrived in Falmouth, Maine—soon to be renamed Portland. Falmouth had been bombarded and burnt to the ground by the British in 1775, but was being rebuilt from the ruins. Peleg, commanding general of American forces in Massachusetts's District of Maine during the war, had been wounded, taken prisoner, escaped, and continued the fight against British encroachment on the northeastern frontier. After the war, he, like so many other veterans, saw opportunity for a new, prosperous life in Maine, and in 1785 he began building in the promising seaport. The house was completed in 1786. To it Peleg and Elizabeth brought their six children: Charles, Zilpah (mother of the poet), Elizabeth, John, Lucia, and Henry (called Harry). Four more Wadsworth children were born there: George, Alexander, Samuel, and Peleg, Jr.

Peleg located his house, along with a barn and a store, on what was then called Back (now Congress) Street, on the outskirts of the waterfront settlement. Back Street, a principal road used by traders to bring goods to market, was a perfect place to set up shop. In the spring of 1787 Peleg expanded his Maine holdings when he acquired 7,800 acres between the Saco and Great Ossipee rivers in what would become the Town of Hiram. By 1795 he had built Wadsworth Hall where his son, Charles, lived to superintend substantial farming and lumbering operations. Peleg and Elizabeth would eventually move there, leaving the house in Portland to their daughters.

In 1792 Peleg, an active participant in Portland's town government, was elected a senator in the Massachusetts legislature and then became Cumberland County's first representative to the United States Congress, an office he held for fourteen consecutive years.

When Congress was in session, he was in Philadelphia and, later, Washington. His role in the Revolutionary War—comrade-at-arms with George Washington, Paul Revere, and the Marquis de Lafayette—and his service in forming America's first government made patriotism more than an abstract ideal in the Wadsworth family: it was a fact of daily life, a part of the family fabric, encompassing children and grandchildren alike.

While Peleg pursued his political career and business enterprise in Hiram, Elizabeth ran the Portland household, guiding their children into adulthood. By 1797 Charles was married and Zilpah, age nineteen, and Elizabeth (called Eliza), eighteen, were cultured and refined young women whose favorite pastimes (when not helping at home) were reading, writing letters, playing the spinet, and drawing. John, age sixteen, would go on to Harvard College. Lucia, age thirteen, and Henry (called Harry), twelve, attended school in Portland. The four youngest boys made up the rest of Elizabeth's charges. In a letter-journal written in 1797, Zilpah provided a vivid vignette of the Wadsworth family, who had gathered on a Sunday evening in the front parlor.

There sits Mama in her lolling chair by the fire. [Eliza] is playing on the piano "Ye Tribes of Adam Join." John and Lucia are singing at the back of her chair. George, Alexander, and Sam are singing in different parts of the room. Little Peleg is stepping about the floor surveying one and another. Charles is sitting at the table with me. He was writing. His pen dropt from his fingers, and he listens to the music. Harry is reading beside me, you know he is always self collected. . . . I have been singing as I wrote. . . . Ten children! What a circle! I should like to know what are Mama's thoughts as she looks around on us.[4]

The Parlor appears today much as it did circa 1886 when photographed by Jackson and Kinney. Treasured family heirlooms include the 1801 engraving of George Washington by Edward Savage and lolling chairs by the Radford brothers, Portland cabinetmakers.

Zilpah found pleasure and relaxation in writing, and her letters and journals provide a charming glimpse of her girlhood. She and Eliza were "sweet girls" with "an unaffected softness of manners" and enjoyed a busy social life. Zilpah was "tall, attractive, with dark hair, lively blue eyes" and a "blooming" complexion. The prevailing interest of Portland's young women was Portland's young men, who were "as plenty as apples in autumn."[5] None of them aroused Zilpah and Eliza Wadsworth's interest, however, until the 1799 arrival of tall, attractive, twenty-three-year-old Stephen Longfellow IV, a Harvard graduate seeking a career in law.

Stephen Longfellow was born in Gorham, the town to which his grandfather and father (Stephen II and Stephen III) had moved following Falmouth's bombardment. His grandfather had been Falmouth's first schoolmaster and filled many important civic offices. His father, one of Gorham's leading citizens, served as representative and senator in the Massachusetts legislature, and as a judge. Stephen was himself an imposing young man: serious, ambitious, and prudent with his money and his time. The young lawyer became a "favorite" of the Wadsworth sisters, and he reciprocated their interest. One observer asked Zilpah, "Which is it—you [or Eliza] . . . that he is partial to?" Zilpah confided to her diary, "I really think myself the most unlikely . . . to engage his heart."[6] She was not wrong; when Stephen declared himself it was to Eliza.

Letters written by Eliza during the summer of 1800 indicate that she and Stephen had an understanding. In October 1801 the young couple's miniatures were painted, probably as gifts for one another, tokens of their mutual affection and commitment.[7] Eliza, however, had begun the decline from tubercular consumption that would cause her death on August 1, 1802. Zilpah devoted herself to nursing her sister and with Stephen watched by her bedside.

Before her death Eliza bequeathed to Zilpah her most cherished possession, a lock of George Washington's hair. In December 1799, the death of America's first and most revered president had produced great national mourning. Eliza wrote to her father asking for a copy of the *Dead March* composed for Washington's funeral or a scrap of Washington's handwriting, adding, "Papa had he hair? A lock of that . . . I should value more highly still." Peleg shared Eliza's request with Martha Washington, who sent him a lock of her beloved husband's hair. In an undated note Eliza wrote, "I wish it may be preserved in our own family while it can be safe. Some years hence . . . if Maine is a separate state . . . I had rather it would be preserved among its treasures."[8] This prophetic concern for the future of Maine (which became a state in 1820), this sense of connection to America's founding, and this under-

This gold locket is inscribed "Washington's Hair. / Given by / Mrs. Washington / to / Miss Eliza Wadsworth. / April 5th 1800 / Henry W. Longfellow. / 1850."

Zilpah and Stephen Longfellow acquired a large dinner service of fashionable transfer-printed pearlware by the British firm Henshall and Company. The poet described the "willow pattern," seen in this detail of a plate, in his poem Kéramos.

standing that future generations would need tangible links to their own history was characteristic of the family. Such acts of historical foresight would be repeated by other Wadsworths and Longfellows in decades to come. Today, Eliza's treasure rests in the collections of the Maine Historical Society.

Eliza also, in a sense, bequeathed to Zilpah something else of great value: her intended, Stephen Longfel-low, whom Zilpah had long loved. On the evening of January 1, 1804, Stephen and Zilpah were married in the parlor where Eliza had died. The young couple's wedding gifts included a table service of English earthenware. Many years later, in his poem *Kéramos*, their son Henry would recall "The willow pattern that we knew / In childhood, with its bridge of blue / Leading to unknown thoroughfares"—one of many images he used to suggest how the hopes for the future were always joined to uncertainty.[9] Indeed, within a year the early happiness of the young couple was marred by another family tragedy: the death of Zilpah's brother Harry, who had set out to prove himself in the new United States Navy. He joined the squadron in the Mediterranean Sea to subdue the Barbary pirates, who had been preying on American shipping. It was one of the earliest demonstrations of American might on the international stage, and the battle of Tripoli became famous. Harry was second in command of a vessel loaded with explosives whose mission was to sneak into the harbor and destroy the enemy's gunboats. His ship, however, exploded prematurely. Harry's death affected the entire family deeply, and Zilpah would soon memorialize him in the naming of her second son Henry Wadsworth.

Domestic life, however, went on in the face of such sadness. In April 1805 the artist William King visited Portland advertising his services to "do silhouettes."[10] The newlyweds, Stephen and Zilpah Longfellow, and Peleg and Elizabeth Wadsworth took advantage of the opportunity. Zilpah's silhouette depicts a young woman with her hair fashionably dressed in a bun with a small braid over her forehead.

The Longfellows

Zilpah long held the opinion that "women never appear . . . so much in the line of their duty as when they are married and bringing up children."[11] Entering quickly and fully into that role, she became the mother of her first child in 1805, named Stephen after his father. Henry Wadsworth Longfellow was born February 27, 1807, in a house on Fore Street, the home of Stephen's sister, Tabitha, and her shipmaster husband, John Stephenson. Tabitha had taken the couple in while her husband was on a voyage.

In the spring of 1807 Peleg refused re-election to Congress and by October he and Elizabeth were ready to move permanently to Wadsworth Hall. Their house in town was offered to the young Longfellows. Zilpah's sister, Lucia, lived with them and would prove a necessary helpmate to Zilpah in the raising of the Longfellow children. By 1819 Stephen and Zilpah were the parents of eight, who composed the verse: *Stephen and Henry / Elizabeth and Anne / Alex and Mary / Ellen and Sam.* Zilpah described Henry as "an active rogue" who "fatigues everyone in the house," for "nothing will do for [him] but jumping and dancing."[12]

In later years Henry would become aware that history also permeated his family's home. Above the parlor mantle, unmoving from its place of honor, was Edward Savage's 1801 engraving of George Washington (after Gilbert Stuart's Landsdowne portrait). There was also the lock of Washington's hair; the sword and musket and stories of his grandfather's Revolutionary War experiences; and the sea exploits of his brave uncle and namesake.[13] During America's federal period, educators believed children should be taught patriotism and morality along with reading, writing, and arithmetic. Henry had the advantage of knowing that the founding of America and its struggle for sovereignty were vivid aspects of his family history. In his Wadsworth line, for instance, he descended from nine *Mayflower* passengers, including John and Priscilla Mullins Alden. Priscilla's response to John's proposal of marriage for Captain Miles Standish—"Why don't you speak for yourself, John?"—was oral history in the family, which Henry would later make unforgettable in his poem *The Courtship of Miles Standish* (1858).[14] His sensitivity to history also made his own personal experience more memorable and charged. One of his earliest memories was of the War of 1812: the battle of the American brig *Enterprise* with the British brig *Boxer* in 1813, off the Maine coast. It was an American

Zilpah Wadsworth Longfellow appears as a stylish young mother in her silhouette, cut by the artist William King in 1805.

victory, but both the British and American captains were killed. For many Mainers, opposed to the war in the first place, these deaths symbolized a basic brotherhood between the two countries. The captains were brought to Portland where they were buried side-by-side with great ceremony in Eastern Cemetery. In one of his most famous poems, *My Lost Youth* (1877), the poet wrote,

> *I remember the sea-fight far away,*
> *How it thundered o'er the tide!*
> *And the dead captains, as they lay*
> *In their graves, o'erlooking the tranquil bay,*
> *Where they in battle died.*[15]

Henry and his siblings enjoyed a happy childhood. Nurtured by a conscientious father, an intelligent mother, and vigilant Aunt Lucia, they were required to perform their youthful duties, but allowed the joys of childhood. Anne, Henry's younger sister, remembered how "books and satchels were the ornaments of the parlor table in the evenings, and silence the motto, till the lessons were learned—then fun and games were not wanting, and when they grew too fast . . . for the parlor, the old kitchen rang with our shouts and glee."[16] The Longfellow children were expected to be "regular at meals, [to] rise early" and "to get their lessons well." During one of Stephen's regular absences from home, Zilpah described their offspring as "pretty-well and tolerably good. Sometimes there is an outbreaking of an unruly spirit. Is not that," the witty Zilpah mused, "original sin?"[17]

Stephen was often absent, traveling throughout Maine to court sessions and in 1814 to Boston as Portland's representative to the Massachusetts General Court. After Maine's statehood in 1820, Stephen represented Portland in the state legislature and then served

Stephen Longfellow sat for his portrait in 1824 while a Congressman in Washington, D.C. Painted by Charles Bird King, one of America's leading artists, the portrait has always hung in the parlor.

Anna M. Bucknam's watercolor view of Congress Street depicts Portland 1820-1825 as the capital of Maine. To the right are the original State House and Cumberland County Courthouse; the large brick Portland Academy, where Henry Longfellow studied, is to the left. The Wadsworth-Longfellow House is located two blocks beyond the First Parish Church, whose steeple is visible.

in the United States Congress from 1823 to 1825. Throughout his busy life, he played significant roles in social and educational organizations, including the Portland Benevolent Society (founder and secretary, 1803-1849) and Bowdoin College (trustee, 1817-1836). In 1822, with Maine Supreme Court justice Prentiss Mellen and Maine's Governor William King, he helped found the Maine Historical Society, the third oldest state historical society after Massachusetts and New York. Stephen was president of the Society in 1834, the same year Henry served as its librarian. They remained members throughout their lives. The close connection between the Longfellow family and the Society, together with the family's deep investment in American history, would ultimately lead to the gift of the Wadsworth-Longfellow House to the Maine Historical Society and the establishment of its permanent headquarters.

Zilpah, like her mother before her, stayed at home to tend to their family. Her constitution was intolerant of Portland's cold and damp air, and the rigors of bearing eight children left her in precarious health. Aunt Lucia ran the house—cooking, sewing, knitting—and managed the entire family. Although essentially housebound, Zilpah was not detached from the wider world; her reading and correspondence with Stephen kept her informed. "Remember my seclusion" and "Do enlighten me a little," she advised him when asking for details about his activities. From Washington he sent news of congressional deliberations. In response, intelligent, strong-minded Zilpah did not hesitate to share her own thinking, even when it disagreed with her husband's. When Stephen stated his position in favor of capital punishment, she replied, "Whence any man or body of men can derive authority to take life I have yet to learn." Deeply spiritual and a liberal Unitarian in her religious persuasion, in her later years she confided to

This small watercolor, by Ann Hall, depicts Henry Wadsworth Longfellow as a young man.

ΑΝΑΛΕΚΤΑ ῾ΕΛΛΗΝΙΚΑ ΜΕΙΖΟΝΑ.

SIVE

COLLECTANEA GRÆCA MAJORA.

As a young teen, Henry Longfellow studied several foreign languages. This copy of Analekta Hellenika Meizona, sive, Collectanea Graeca Majora *bears the pencil inscription "Henry W. Longfellow / Portland Academy / October / 1821."*

her daughter, Mary, "the longer I live less important do mere forms of worship appear to me."[18]

Henry was raised by a father whose ambition was not "to accumulate wealth for my children, but to cultivate their minds in the best possible manner and to imbue them with correct moral, political, and religious principals." Zilpah echoed these sentiments and the ideals of class and New England restraint that underlay them.[19]

As a youth Henry was "a lively boy, with brown or chestnut hair, blue eyes, a delicate complexion and rosy cheeks; sensitive, impressionable; active, eager, impetuous, often impatient; quick-tempered, but as quickly appeased; kind-hearted and affectionate—the sunlight of the house."[20] Elijah Kellogg, Longfellow's schoolmate at Portland Academy, remembered "there was a frankness about him that won you at once. He looked you square in the face. . . . He had no relish for rude sports, but loved to bathe in a little creek on the border of Deering's Oaks."[21] His favorite book as a child was

The Arabian Nights, but for Henry, like all his siblings, stimulation was everywhere. Even late in life his youngest brother, Samuel, had vivid memories of their play in the old barn, memories "of rare visits to that mysterious dove-chamber, so like it seemed to the small places one gets into in dreams."[22]

Henry's love of books and his active intelligence found early expression in poetry. He is said to have written his first poems at a table in his mother's room.[23] Henry was thirteen when with "trembling and misgiving" he submitted his poem *The Battle of Lovell's Pond* to the *Portland Gazette*. It had, not surprisingly, a historical theme: a battle with the Indians in 1725 in Fryeburg, Maine—a story he probably heard from his Grandfather Wadsworth in nearby Hiram. Signing his poem simply as "Henry," only he and his ten-year-old sister, Anne, knew of his daring try for publication. Their joy at its appearance in the November 17, 1820, issue was short-lived when a family friend pronounced it "stiff, remarkably stiff! And it is all borrowed, every line of it."[24] He would, however, eventually become a master of supple verse forms and a borrower of great sophistication.

Henry was also attuned to the world around him. Throughout his childhood the city of Portland grew and encroached upon the house Peleg Wadsworth had built on the edge of town. Shipyards, the county court house, artisans' shops, the Observatory and Fort Sumner on Munjoy Hill, ropewalks, and wharves were all within an easy distance. Though Henry would eventually become identified with the gentility of his mansion in Cambridge, the hard-working vitality of Portland captured his imagination. In later years his poetry, always in search of time-softened memories, would return to the sights of his childhood. *The Ropewalk* (1858) provides a famous image of the poetic process.

As the Spinners to the end
Downward go and reascend,
Gleam the long threads in the sun;
While within this brain of mine
Cobwebs brighter and more fine
By the busy wheel are spun.[25]

In the autumn of 1821 Henry passed his entrance examinations for Bowdoin College. Because he was not yet fifteen his parents kept him at home for a year of study before allowing him to move to Brunswick to enter as a member of Bowdoin's sophomore class—a class that included both the writer Nathaniel Hawthorne and future President of the United States, Franklin Pierce.

The following decades brought changes to the Wadsworth-Longfellow House and its occupants. Most notable were Henry's literary success and Anne's marriage and widowhood. On November 26, 1832, Anne married George Washington Pierce, a classmate and close friend of Henry's, who had studied law in Stephen Longfellow's office. In October 1835 George died of typhus, and Anne returned to her parents' home to face her loss—compounded by the death of her sixteen-year-old sister, Ellen, from the same disease.

Anne Longfellow Pierce

Anne Longfellow Pierce lived on in the Portland house with her parents and Aunt Lucia. As a young widow "sad beyond description," she forced herself to "sit downstairs with the others more . . . and talk more to them but generally without feeling any interest or half the time knowing what I'm talking about." Her greatest comfort was her mother. "I love so to be . . . with my good old mother—she talks with me from morning till night of my own dear George." How wise of Zilpah to talk to Anne about her "dear George" and the brief happiness they had shared in what Anne would look back on as "my little life."[26] Anne healed herself by staying involved with the extended family, creating a flower garden behind the house, running the household, and following the life and career of her dearest brother, who was becoming increasingly famous.

In the years that followed, Henry and Fanny, and later their children, made annual visits to Portland, usually in the summer. By 1851 the household that greeted them had been seriously altered. Stephen Longfellow died on August 3, 1849, after more than a decade of "bad days." Zilpah died on March 13, 1851.[27] When Henry received the news of her death by telegraph, he left immediately for Portland. "In the chamber where I last took leave of her . . . a sense of peace came over me, as if there had been no shock or jar in nature, but a harmonious close to a long life."[28] Zilpah bequeathed her half of the Wadsworth-Longfellow House to Anne. When Lucia died in 1864, she too left her share to Anne, whose increasing responsibility for the house became a legal fact.

In this period, fire—Anne's ever-present fear—also took its toll. The house was brick, but the barn that Peleg built was attached to the house by a wooden ell and outbuildings (one of which housed the privy). In 1849 a nearby stable caught fire, and Anne described its effect: "Coals of fire were literally showered down upon our roof . . . and the whole street & air was full of burning cinders. . . . Lucia [was] soon at the cistern. Alex. . . upon the roof. . . . What would have become of us if he had been out of town? [The] old roof must certainly have caught."[29] She was thankful the Longfellows' old barn "was out of the range of the wind." Inevitably, however, the barn did burn in March 1851.

Joseph Greenleaf Cole captured the youthful Anne Longfellow Pierce in his oil portrait, one of several family pictures to decorate the house. A stylish and engaging young lady, Anne is depicted at the time of her 1832 marriage to George Washington Pierce, Henry's long-time friend and Bowdoin College classmate.

Anne was surprised that she was "not at all frightened . . . when beholding that old barn—the terror of my nights for years actually burning before my eyes."[30]

Through it all the house endured, and remained a busy place. Alexander—a noisy, booted, cigar-smoking, late-night-keeping presence—still lived at home. As a civil engineer for the United States Coast Survey, he charted the shoreline and harbors of New England. After he married Elizabeth Clapp Porter in 1851, they stayed for a winter before moving into their own Portland home. To Anne "no gentleman in the house seems

Mary King Longfellow photographed her aunt, Anne Longfellow Pierce, in 1897 in the Summer Dining Room. Anne is seen with her portrait and a writing desk used as a sideboard.

to make no family."[31] The same could be said for children, but there were many in her life—nieces and nephews and the children of relatives or friends from distant Maine towns who boarded with her in order to attend Portland schools. Most particularly, she was involved with the children of her troubled brother, Stephen, and his wife, Marianne, who often brought their youngest offspring for the day, making extra work. In 1850 when Marianne divorced the alcoholic Stephen for lack of support and adultery, Marianne's father demanded that the Longfellows provide support for his daughter's five children.

In 1850 Anne took legal guardianship of ten-year-old Henry, his famous uncle's namesake. Anne was forty when Hen, as she called him, came to live with her, and she confided to Mary that her responsibility for him was daunting but "presents itself so strongly as a duty."[32] She gave Hen birthday parties, allowed school friends to visit for noisy play, listened to his prayers, and filled his Christmas stocking. In late nineteenth-century photographs, Anne is an old woman, her waistline lost to age, her dress severe. The expression on her face hints at stress and, interestingly, diffidence. Her love of children, however, remained alive.

Anne lived eighty-seven of her ninety years in the house she called "dear old home." "[I] am happier here than anywhere. An affectionate presence seems to enfold me here. . . . A benediction will ever rest on us children under the old roof tree . . . so long as memory of our dear parents lives within us." Her feelings were shared by the two generations of Wadsworth and Longfellow children who had lived there and later visited. Her uncle, John Wadsworth, observed: "[I need to] maintain some kind of connection with the old homestead, a kind of moral chain of communion, even if the links be sometimes a year long."[33] Anne called their visits "house vacations." Henry helped maintain the Portland household by providing regular financial assistance to Anne throughout her life.[34]

Anne died in 1901, nineteen years after the death of her beloved Henry. During her final years she arranged for the future of her "dear old home." In 1895 she executed a deed for her bequest of the house to the Maine Historical Society. A new headquarters for their collections was to be built on the site of the barn. The house was to be preserved as a "Longfellow Memorial" with the two first-floor front rooms "kept with appropriate articles for a memorial of the Home of Longfellow." After Anne's death in January 1901, the Society accepted her bequest, fulfilling her wish that the house become not only a shrine to the brother she valued for his abiding friendship and support, his accomplishments and fame, but also as a memorial to the family that reared him.[35]

The Wadsworth-Longfellow House appears circa 1907 with the new Maine Historical Society library, designed by Alexander Wadsworth Longfellow, Jr., the colonial-revival Boston architect and poet's nephew.

The 2000-2002 reproduction of door and window blinds and documented paint colors contributed to the historical accuracy of the Wadsworth-Longfellow House.

The Wadsworth-Longfellow House:
Its History and Restoration

LAURA FECYCH SPRAGUE

THE Wadsworth-Longfellow House survives with great historical integrity largely because of the preservation philosophy of Anne Longfellow Pierce. She was keenly aware of her brother's fame, the public's interest in his boyhood home, and the early characteristics of their grandparents' house. A National Historic Landmark, it is a notable example of colonial and federal American residences preserved by members of the Longfellow family. For example, from 1837 until 1882, Henry Wadsworth Longfellow occupied Craigie House, a colonial masterpiece built in 1759, which served as George Washington's headquarters during the Revolutionary War. Anne often visited him there. In 1851 Anne Pierce visited "the ancestral acres in Byfield, . . . the Old Longfellow House, yet occupied, as it always has been by one of the name and family."[36]

As early as 1850, Anne Pierce repeatedly referred to the "old fashioned" quality of her family's Portland seat, which she and her family treasured as "the old original." She took a conservative approach to any modification: "I do hate to change any thing so much."[37] Her decorating decisions reflected the Victorian aesthetic, but always kept the historic nature of the building in mind.

Anne Pierce, with the encouragement and support of her siblings, redecorated most of the rooms follow-ing the death of her mother in 1851 when Henry was at the height of his career. The public learned about the house through a descriptive, illustrated chapter in the *Longfellow Remembrance Book*, published in 1888. That interior design remained in place until Anne Pierce's death in 1901. The house was then refurbished by the Maine Historical Society—with guidance of the Longfellow family—to fulfill its new role as a public memorial to Henry Wadsworth Longfellow. It opened to the public in the summer of 1901 as Maine's first—and one of America's earliest—historic house museums.[38] The centennial restoration of 2000-2002 recreated the family's mid nineteenth-century choices. With historic paint colors; custom reproduction wall-papers, floor coverings, and textiles; and conserved family furnishings, the house today appears as close as possible to the one the famed poet knew.

In 1784 Adjutant General Peleg Wadsworth pur-chased a lot of roughly one-and-one-half acres. Narrow but deep, it ran north one-half mile to Back Cove. His two-story wood-frame store and barn were the first structures to be built. The architectural style and mate-rial for the house indicated Wadsworth's taste and place in society. While brick-ended wood-frame houses were built during the colonial period, Wadsworth's fully brick residence was Portland's first when it was begun

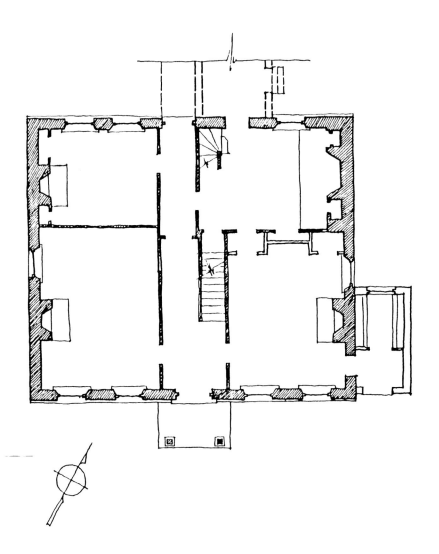

The house was designed on the central-hall plan. The four rooms on the first floor correspond to four bed chambers on the second floor.

in 1785. Originally constructed with a steep gabled roof, its symmetrical design of five bays centered on the main door with projecting portico, was derived from neoclassical English architecture.[39]

Wadsworth commissioned John Nichols, a Portland brick mason, with the construction which took two years. The brick was imported from Philadelphia. Wadsworth's choice of the central-hall plan provided conveniences unknown in many of Portland's colonial central-chimney residences. Four chimneys on the exterior walls provided fireplaces in all eight rooms, four over four. The large central hall, running the depth of the house to the back door, allowed easy access throughout the house for this family of twelve. By federal American standards, the size and arrangement was generous, especially in the separation of public and private spaces.

Facing south, two parlors overlooked the street, with the largest parlor to the west. The site of special events, the best parlor also served the Wadsworths daily for reading, writing, conversation, and music. The smaller parlor or sitting room to the east offered great flexibility in its use for dining or entertaining. At the rear of the house, a small room was tucked behind the best parlor, and the kitchen was handy to the work spaces—the ell or "porch" as the family called it, wood house, well, barn, and privy. On the second floor were four sleeping chambers, with the best chamber over the parlor bearing the highest level of ornamentation. The family's second-best chamber was also at the front of the house over the sitting room. The smaller back chambers faced north and were cooler in summer.

The residence served the Wadsworths from 1786 until 1807. When General and Mrs. Wadsworth retired to Wadsworth Hall, the young Longfellow family took occupancy. Upon his death in 1829, Peleg Wadsworth bequeathed the residence to Zilpah and Lucia.[40]

Continuity and Change

What the Wadsworths considered fashionable in 1785 was outdated by early nineteenth-century standards, and Zilpah and Stephen began to redecorate and update the house. Their renovations not only improved accommodations for their family but also expressed their preferences for the neoclassical taste. Although the Longfellows did not have an "independent fortune," as Zilpah called it, they aspired to the styles set by New England's elite. Portland's merchant princes had chosen four-square, three-story brick dwellings beginning with the 1800-1801 construction of the Hugh McLellan House (now the Portland Museum of Art). In addition to the Wadsworth-Longfellow House, Congress Street was the fashionable address for the elegant residences of Asa Clapp, Matthew Cobb, and Edward Preble, the area's wealthiest residents.[41]

In September 1814 a fire in the kitchen chimney destroyed the gable roof. The family immediately planned to "put on another story and L [ell], which will make a $500 job but the House will be better than it was." New window sashes with large six-over-six panes or lights replaced the old twelve-over-twelve design. For a modest investment, the home of the Wadsworth-Longfellows now resembled the houses of their wealthy, sophisticated neighbors (particularly Edward Preble, commodore of the United States Navy, directly next door). The third floor included seven chambers for Lucia Wadsworth and the eight Longfellow children.[42]

Throughout the early nineteenth century, the Longfellows' renewed their interior with "modern conveniences" to achieve greater physical comfort as well as improved social status. Paint freshened walls and woodwork and new fashionable wallpaper enlivened at least three principal rooms. For example, the 1786 hall wallpaper, damaged during lengthy third-floor construction, was replaced in 1815 by a pattern of leafy bamboo poles to create a light and spacious hall. The hall was further ornamented with a stair carpet in 1836. As early as 1826, a bell system was in place, which helped summon family members and household help. Zilpah's struggle to warm the house was aided to some degree by a central wood-burning furnace. Physical and written evidence of the use of stoves throughout the house is matched by references to fire and dangerous configurations of stove pipes.[43]

The kitchen saw regular modifications between 1786 and the mid 1850s to ease the tedious process of hearth cooking, brick-oven baking, water collection, and laundry. A pump in the kitchen reduced the number of back-breaking trips to the well. The family built a brick cistern in the basement to hold runoff from the roof, and by 1850 water was no longer collected from the well.

Activities on cloudy days, in the evenings, and in winter were eased by argand and solar lamps, which were known for the intensity of their light. Oil-burning, blown-glass ceiling lamps were installed in the halls during the early decades of the nineteenth century.[44]

One of the remarkable features of the occupancy of Anne Pierce and Lucia Wadsworth is that while they made decorative changes, the mechanical systems remained largely unchanged. By the mid nineteenth century, the luster of Henry's literary career and the antiquarian nature of the house found expression in the building's preservation. Here Anne Pierce's attitude departed from her parents' desire for the "comforts of home." Beginning in 1849, other Portland residents installed piped natural gas and plumbed for running water, especially water closets, but Anne cherished "the old original" where she felt as "snug . . . as a snail bug." The "modern" conveniences of her childhood

The hall provided easy access throughout the house for the large Wadsworth and Longfellow family. Reproductions of the French rococo-revival wallpaper first installed around 1850, a painted canvas floorcloth, and a stair carpet created a stylish but practical entryway.

became the antiquated comforts of her old age. Mary King Longfellow, Anne's niece, documented simple aspects of the interior with a series of photographs in the 1890s. A humble kitchen sink, pump, and dish drainer would rarely merit a photographer's attention, but these rich, antiquarian elements interested Mary King Longfellow. Anne Pierce held the last city permit for a privy in Portland.[45]

Following the deaths of Stephen and Zilpah Longfellow, a major decorative cycle renewed the interior. Anne preserved what she called "the ancient" character of the house while updating it according to current tastes. There is ample documentation for these changes, including wallpaper fragments; family letters, journals, and other accounts; historic photographs; and the extraordinary collection of family furnishings. They all contribute to a modern understanding of the decisions Anne Pierce made and served as the foundation for the centennial restoration.[46]

Exterior

The Longfellows separated their house lot into formal and domestic spaces by the use of fences. Across the front a simple iron fence gave a formal presence to the main entry. A solid wooden-board fence set off the service area and drying yard to the east. Large elm trees shaded the yard along Congress Street. Today's high iron fence and plantings do not reproduce the Longfellows' domestic grounds, but are a modern interpretation of the colonial-revival garden plan of landscape architect Myron Lamb, installed in the 1920s.[47]

The façade's first floor featured exterior blinds or shutters in place by 1867, when the earliest known photograph was taken. Blinds were also used on the upper stories, but only on the side and back of the house. The front door retains its original brass knocker and a door bell was added in the early nineteenth century. "Double" or storm windows were in use by 1851, an early Maine example.[48]

First Floor

Hall

In the front hall the walls retain their original eighteenth-century wainscot paneling; the upper plaster wall was decorated with wallpaper beginning in 1786. The influential American architect Alexander Jackson Downing suggested new styles and decoration of residences in *The Architecture of Country Houses* (1850). The hall's costly French rococo-revival paper, featuring large cartouches, illustrates "the enhanced architectural effect which may be given a plain room, by covering the walls with paper of a suitable style." Anne Pierce's choice may have been inspired by the rococo-revival paper Henry and Fanny selected for the Craigie House parlor in 1844. Anne's design was particularly sophisticated with the use of two alternating rolls. Borders representing architectural molding and leaves at the ceiling and wainscot further defined the room.[49]

As early as 1841 Zilpah Longfellow discussed the purchase of a new floor covering for the hall. A painted canvas carpet or floorcloth had been a popular choice from the eighteenth century because of its durable varnished surface. "Why everybody has it," her family urged. "Is that a good reason?" she replied. After Zilpah's death, "a painted floorcloth was put down on the front entry which with two nice handsome mats give the old place quite the look of a lady's premises without materially changing the entry," reported Anne in 1852. Anne's design featured bold oak leaves enclosed in diamonds. A woven runner, secured by brass rods, carpeted the stairs.[50] An elegant blown-and-engraved glass fluid lamp illuminated the space. (The Longfellows' oil lighting fixtures were wired for electricity by the Society in 1903.)

Parlor

The parlor was always the best room, used regularly by both families as well as for special formal occasions. For example, Zilpah wrote during her childhood of the reading and musical events that occurred here. This room is where Eliza Wadsworth died in 1802 and where the Wadsworth and Longfellow daughters were married. Furnished with family portraits, landscape paintings, engravings, and stylish furniture, it appears much as it did after Longfellow's death in 1882, when it was photographed for the *Longfellow Remembrance Book*. By this date, some furnishings had achieved heirloom status, including the colonial Boston chairs inherited from Stephen's parents, the 1808 Portland lolling chairs, and the 1801 Edward Savage print of George Washington in its historic location over the mantle. Two images of Evangeline, the heroine of Henry's epic poem, also decorated the parlor. The 1855 engraving by James Faed was, according to Anne Pierce, "the first one made after the Poem came out." Several different pianos were integral parlor furnishings over the years. The poet's Bellisent flute from Paris and early American music books with family annotations are in the collec-

tion. In the corner, Anne nurtured an orange tree that had "grown old with age."[51]

In the parlor, as in the rest of the house, the woodwork is painted in what was then in favor, "quiet, neutral tints"—fawn, drab, stone color, and gray—"pleasing and harmonious" colors. In both the parlor and the sitting room, polychrome or two-toned paints highlight the architectural details of the moldings and doors. The high-gloss oil-based paints used in 2000-2002 simulate the shiny, lead-based paint long favored by Americans.[52]

Sitting Room

In 1853 Anne converted the smaller front parlor into a sitting room for daily use, selecting an example of wallpaper found in New England's most fashionable houses. The room had served previously as a dining room from 1807 when the Longfellows furnished it with a handsome sideboard and dining tables. In 1815 it became Stephen's law office and a new side entrance and vestibule were built to divert clients from the family's hall. Henry often found the entry a quiet place to read, write, and study. In November 1825 Stephen moved his office to Court Street, and the room was again remodelled for dining. The vestibule was converted for storage of china and housewares. Henry regretted that the little room he recalled so fondly had been transformed: "—no soft poetic ray has irradiated my heart—since the Goths and Vandals swept over the Rubicon of the 'front entry' and turned the Sanctum Sanctorum of the 'Little Room' into a China Closet."[53]

An innovative sideboard-bookcase dominates the room. With a center drawer that folds down to form a

The parlor, restored in 2000-2002 to its Victorian appearance, features polychrome paint colors to highlight the woodwork, French wallpaper, and a woven wall-to-wall Brussels carpet.

The sitting room, with its sideboard-bookcase in a recessed alcove, is furnished with family furniture, portraits, and prints. The mid nineteenth-century paint, wallpaper, and carpeting were reproduced in 2000-2002.

writing space, it ably served Stephen Longfellow in place of a more traditional desk. The sideboard's upper bookcase dates from 1815, and housed part of Stephen's extensive law library.[54] Charles O. Cole's 1842 unfinished oil portrait of the poet and Eastman Johnson's charcoal drawing of Anne Pierce decorate the walls. According to Anne Pierce, her father accepted the French mantle clock as payment for services rendered by a cash-strapped client after the Embargo of 1807. The symbolism of the phoenix, which surmounts the clock, was not lost on the Longfellows, who helped Portland rebuild its Revolutionary War losses. Portland embraced the phoenix as its symbol in 1786.

Seated at a favorite window in the sitting room, Anne Pierce is surrounded by books and plants. Her father's French clock is on the mantel. The fireplace had been updated with a coal grate and decorative tiles.

Summer Dining Room

The small room behind the parlor, a place for quiet reflection, was where Henry wrote his poem *The Rainy Day*. During the 1840s, it served as an office for his brother Alexander, but after he left the house, it was converted for use as a summer dining room. In March 1853, Anne wrote "of the charming paper" brother Sam provided. "The paint is to be oak [grained], very light and the back entry to match—it all needs the renovation badly, but I do hate to change any thing so much."[55] Victorian publications recommended this painted finish. "The great advantage which grained woodwork has over that which is simply painted white, is that it is so easily kept clean. . . . The grained surface being made smooth by varnishing, does not readily become soiled." This durable decoration has survived remarkably well for 150 years.[56]

The northern exposure with a view to the garden offered cool, welcome relief from the noisy street. As the fireplace was not needed, the fireplace opening was closed up with a fireboard covered with wallpaper, a popular nineteenth-century technique. The room was furnished with mahogany drop-leaf dining tables and rosewood-grained side chairs. Photographs show the mahogany writing desk used by the poet in a new role as a sideboard. New additions included an oil-burning lamp with counterweights that allowed it to be raised and lowered. Anne completed the room with a straw carpet, a popular floor covering. Important family tablewares include a colonial silver tankard made by John Butler, a creamware pitcher made circa 1800 in memory of George Washington, and an English table service. The pitcher, inscribed "Washington in Glory / America in Tears," was used to serve lemonade on the Fourth of July. Even after it was cracked, it still made "its annual appearance on the day of National rejoicing."[57]

This view depicts the summer dining room as it appeared in 1886. On this desk Henry wrote his poem The Rainy Day; *it was also used in his sister's dining room as a sideboard.*

Rear Hall

In April 1853 Anne "installed wallpaper above the grain-painted woodwork" and described the entry as "much more tidy and lady-like. . . . I have an oil cloth like the front one and upon the whole we look pretty well." The new wallpaper featured ashlar blocks, a pattern resembling masonry that had been fashionable, especially in halls, since colonial times. Anne sought an "old fashioned" design. The wallpaper covered pencil inscriptions by the family dating between 1832 and 1852. Early nineteenth-century leather firebuckets, made by local saddler Aaron Fitz, were handy in case of need as were iron coat hooks. A handsome gothic-revival ceiling lamp illuminated the space.[58]

Kitchen

Much of the kitchen's original configuration survives with its dominant cooking hearth, fireback, and bake oven. The iron fireback, set in 1785 into the firebox, radiated heat to make the large fireplace more efficient. Cast with an image of a codfish, it is a rare example of the work of Joseph Webb of Boston. To Samuel Longfellow, it was a fish "baked in effigy." Here, as in other rooms, the family stayed abreast of technological innovations to ease burdensome chores. Architectural and written evidence reveal many modifications between 1786 and 1853. The arched cupboard dates to the 1826 improvements in the adjoining sitting room. A cook stove was added by at least 1850 when Anne Pierce recorded looking for fuel. Although low and small, it offered conveniences to the Victorian cook not known in hearth cooking. During Anne Pierce's occupancy, a pump was installed to bring running water into the kitchen from the cistern. Photographs by Mary King Longfellow document Anne's modest kitchen with early nineteenth-century painted chairs, oil-cloth table cover, and basic housewares.[59]

Microanalysis documented over fifteen layers of paint on the plaster walls before the first layer of wallpaper was applied in 1853. These many coats refreshed a space quickly soiled by smoke and grease. With the addition of wallpaper, Anne delighted that "the old kitchen is quite fine with its shining flowered walls." Fragments of her paper survive under varnish. Household manuals advised varnishing so the paper could be wiped clean. A glossy greenish-gray woodwork mitigated signs of soil.[60]

The kitchen retains many of its original features, including the open hearth with fireback. Greenish-gray woodwork hid soil; the varnished wallpaper reflected light and was easy to clean.

Joseph Webb, of Boston, Massachusetts, cast this fireback with an image of a codfish. It was installed in the kitchen fireplace when the house was built in 1785-1786. This rare fireback was described as the fish "baked in effigy."

Ell or Porch

To ease access to the well and domestic yard, the Longfellows converted the kitchen's north window into a door in 1807. Attached to the house, the wooden "porch" extended to a wood house, then the barn and privy. Along its western exterior side, a raised wooden walk ran from the rear hall door. Terrified of the risk of fire the wooden ell posed, especially after the barn burned, Anne Pierce decided to make a brick replacement "a precise repetition of the old one." Masons and plasterers were at work in May 1852.[61]

Second Floor

Parlor Chamber or Mother's Room

On the second floor, the southwest room was the best chamber, elegantly decorated and furnished. Plagued by ill health, Zilpah Longfellow spent many hours here. The high-post bedstead with its painted oak-leaf cornice was made for the Longfellows by the Radford Brothers in January 1808. The bright red-and-yellow "Pompeian" bed curtains were the height of fashion that year. The reproduction of the original English cotton was based on the counterpane surviving from the set. Beds were among a household's most costly furnishings throughout the colonial and federal eras. A complete set of bed hangings included head and foot curtains, counterpane or coverlet, inner and outer valances, head cloth, and tester. Combined with the requisite featherbeds, bolsters, and mattresses, the cost of the textiles far exceeded the cabinetmaker's bill for the frame. When a new chest of drawers was sought, the Saco cabinetmakers Cumston and Buckminster provided an elegant veneered example. This stylish federal furniture was used alongside inherited colonial Massachusetts furniture. According to family tradition, the early dressing table and side chairs were brought to Portland by the Wadsworths in 1785. The young Henry used the colonial tea table for writing, as Anne related later in the nineteenth century. Although table tops were often covered with cloths to protect them, this top exhibits considerable wear. The Longfellows updated the woodwork and refurbished the wallpaper. In 1826 they installed the sophisticated French paper—a verdant bower with bright blue trellis—that remained on the walls until 1901.[62]

The parlor chamber or Mother's room was reinstalled in 2000-2002 with reproductions of the original family textiles and wallpaper. The Radford brothers crafted the high-post bed with its painted cornice in 1808. Bed curtains in "Pompeian" colors are a custom reproduction of the Longfellow's English cotton. The French trellis wallpaper was the height of fashion when first hung in 1826.

The guest chamber was the second-best bed chamber. Henry used it during visits to his childhood home; his father and sister Anne died in this room. Its bed and windows are dressed with cotton dimity, and a replica of the original straw matting carpets the floor. Both were popular nineteenth-century furnishing fabrics.

Sitting Room Chamber or Guest Room

The sleeping chamber located over the sitting room, also called the "front room," was made available for guests. In such a large household, however, it was not practical to set aside one of the best chambers only for visitors. Stephen Longfellow died in this room in 1849 and may have had more frequent use of it in his later years as Zilpah's illnesses kept her confined to her chamber across the hall. Anne Pierce also died here in 1901.[63]

Cotton dimity, a ubiquitous nineteenth-century furnishing fabric, decorates the chamber along with reproduction straw matting. The high-post bedstead, attributed to a Portland cabinet shop, is dressed with a full set of bed curtains. In 1808 the Radford brothers made a toilet table, a simple pine frame that when covered with fabric became a stylish dressing table. Watercolors attributed to Ellen or Elizabeth Longfellow, possibly school assignments, decorate the walls. A leather trunk used by the poet during his Europe grand tour between 1826 and 1829 was given to the Society by his daughters in 1903.

Kitchen Chamber

The family referred to the northeast room as the kitchen chamber or back room. A secondary bed chamber, it would have been used by younger members of the Wadsworth and Longfellow families. Readily accessible to the kitchen by way of the rear stairs, the room was more than warmed by heat from the cooking hearth. The Longfellow children reportedly sat at the top of the stairs on Thanksgiving morning, inhaling "delightful odors."[64]

Henry Wadsworth Longfellow II, the poet's nephew, represents another generation who may have used this room. After Hen's parents, Stephen and Marianne Preble Longfellow, were divorced in 1850 and his father died in 1851, his Aunt Anne became his guardian. Hen was the source of constant comment in family correspondence and constant consternation for Anne and Lucia.

The pine child's desk, worn and scribbled with graffiti, dates to the school years of the Longfellow

One of the Longfellow sisters, Elizabeth or Ellen, is believed to have sketched the wreath of flowers. It may be an example of a school assignment.

children. Eighteenth-century French prints of children and maps of places near and far are a few of the many works on paper from the Longfellow family collection. Surveyor Alexander W. Longfellow owned many maps that were given to the house. The ochre walls, gray green woodwork, and brown floor are all documented by paint analysis.

Anne Longfellow Pierce's Chamber

Anne Longfellow Pierce lived many of her ninety years in a small chamber overlooking the garden. After the death of her beloved George Washington Pierce in 1835, Anne returned to her childhood home and the company of her family. Her "mahogany chamber set" was distributed to family members in 1901, but many other family furnishings are exhibited here. Notable are the silhouette of George Washington Pierce and his plaster bust of Lord Byron, the Romantic English writer known for his infamous and daring life who Henry Longfellow admired.[65]

Paint analysis revealed that the walls were painted only twice between 1785 and 1901. The pink replicates the mid nineteenth-century calcimine paint. In this room, removed from Congress Street, Anne was handy to the parlor chamber where she helped care for her mother.

Second-floor Rear Hall

The arrangement of the rear hall with its 1785 stairway to the kitchen and 1815 stair to the third floor allowed children and household help to access rooms without disturbing activities in the front of the house. Glass

La Danse en Rond, *an eighteenth-century French print, is one of a series owned by the family.*

Little Eliza Wadsworth had her name scratched into the wet plaster of her family's new home in 1785-1786.

Anne Longfellow Pierce's chamber was a small room overlooking the garden. The early pink calcimine wall paint and olive-green woodwork were restored in 2000-2002. Family furnishings, including important examples of Maine furniture, decorate the room.

The kitchen chamber, a small back room over the kitchen, was used by the many Wadsworth and Longfellow children. The bright ochre walls, green woodwork, and brown floor were all documented by paint analysis.

panes set into the stair-landing doors provided necessary light to navigate the steep passage. The wall bears a small handprint and the inscription "Eliza Wadsworth," who took advantage of the wet plaster while the interior was being completed in 1786.

Third Floor

"Seven very convenient and pleasant chambers" were built on the third floor in 1815.[66] Lucia Wadsworth occupied the two southeast chambers with a panoramic view over the city, harbor, and islands of Casco Bay. Tradition gives Henry use of the large southwest chamber. The younger boys slept in the northwest chamber and the daughters in the northeast chamber, both with views to Back Cove, Deering's Woods, and Mount Washington. Among the graffiti dating between 1830 and 1857 on one window frame are the inscriptions "how dear is the home of my childhood" and "Friday eve'g July 14th 1837—a magnificent sunset of golden clouds."

The walls were decorated in 1815 with bright green calcimine paint. The paint was still visible when the third-floor rooms were photographed in 1904. At that time, the southwest room, "the poet's sleeping chamber," was furnished with early nineteenth-century Maine furniture. Of note is the bed's counterpane, the only surviving part of the curtains first made in 1808 for the best bed in the parlor chamber on the second floor.

The third-floor chamber, long associated with Henry Wadsworth Longfellow, is seen in a 1904 view taken after the house opened to the public. The original green calcimine paint is still visible.

HENRY WADSWORTH LONGFELLOW long cherished his family residence, the elegant brick house built by his maternal grandparents and lovingly occupied throughout the nineteenth century by the Longfellows. As he wrote in 1854,

We may build more splendid habitations,
Fill our rooms with paintings and with sculpture,
But we cannot
Buy with gold the old associations![67]

Readers' Note

The letters of Stephen and Zilpah Wadsworth Longfellow, and their children, Anne Longfellow Pierce, Mary Longfellow Greenleaf, and Samuel Longfellow are in the archives of the National Park Service, Longfellow National Historic Site, Cambridge, Massachusetts, cited below as LNHS, and quoted with their kind permission.

NOTES

1. Andrew Hilen, ed., *The Letters of Henry Wadsworth Longfellow*, six volumes, (Cambridge, Mass.: The Belknap Press of Harvard University Press, 1966), 1:94-95.

2. Hilen, *Letters*, 1:280.

3. J. D. McClatchy, ed., *Henry Wadsworth Longfellow: Poems and Other Writings* (New York: Library of America, 2000), p. 4.

4. Letter-journal, Zilpah Wadsworth (hereafter cited as ZW) to Nancy Doane, November 29 to December 19, 1797, LNHS.

5. Letter-journal, ZW to Nancy Doane, November 29 to December 19, 1797, LNHS; Abigail May diary, August 23, 1796, Maine Historical Society (hereafter cited as MHS). John Wadsworth to Anne Longfellow Pierce (hereafter cited as ALP), March 15, 1853, LNHS.

6. Diary, ZW, April 25 and June 22, 1799, LNHS.

7. The miniatures are illustrated in Laura Fecych Sprague, ed., *Agreeable Situations: Society, Commerce, and Art in Southern Maine, 1780-1830* (Kennebunk, Me.: The Brick Store Museum, 1987), p. 123.

8. Letters, Eliza Wadsworth, Peleg Wadsworth, and Tobias Lear, January 19, 1800, to April 5, 1800, Miscellaneous Box 5, Folder 5, MHS. The letters and locket were given to MHS by Henry Wadsworth Longfellow heirs in December 1899.

9. McClatchy, *Poems*, p. 643.

10. *Portland Gazette*, April 22, 1805.

11. Letter-journal, ZW to Nancy Doane, April 1, 1797, LNHS.

12. Nathan Goold, quoted the ditty in *The Wadsworth-Longfellow House: Its History and Its Occupants* (Portland, Me.: [Maine Historical Society], 1908), p. 11. ALP may have shared it with him. Letter, Zilpah Wadsworth Longfellow (hereafter cited as ZWL) to Alexander Wadsworth, and Stephen Longfellow (hereafter cited as SL), October 4, 1807, LNHS.

13. Copy of "Directions Written by Aunt Anne, Probably about 1894, No. 3," ex-collection Anne Longfellow Thorp, MHS, gift of Mrs. Bradford Wetherell, 2001.

14. It was first recorded by the Reverend Timothy Alden in 1814. Longfellow probably knew the story from his mother and from Timothy Alden's family record.

15. McClatchy, *Poems*, pp. 337-340.

16. Letter, ALP to George Washington Greene, March 17, 1879, LNHS.

17. Letter, ZWL to Lucia Wadsworth and the children, June 2, 1822, LNHS; ZWL to SL, October 19, 1822, LNHS.

18. Letters, ZWL to SL, October 6, 1820, January 13, 1814, January 28, 1824, and February 13, 1825. ZWL to Mary Longfellow Greenleaf (hereafter cited as MLG), March 10, 1841, LNHS.

19. Ella M. Bangs, *An Historic Mansion: The Wadsworth-Longfellow House, Portland* (Portland, Me.: The Lamson Studio, 1903), pp. 9-10.

20. Bangs, *Historic Mansion*, p. 12. See also George Thornton Edwards, *The Youthful Haunts of Longfellow* (Portland, Me.: George T. Edwards, 1907), pp. 21-22, and Samuel Longfellow, *Memoir and Letters*, three volumes, edited by Joseph May (Boston and New York: Houghton, Mifflin and Company, 1894), 3:296.

21. Bangs, *Historic Mansion*, p. 13, and Samuel Longfellow, "Longfellow's Boyhood," *Longfellow Remembrance Book: A Memorial for the Poet's Reader-Friends* (Boston: D. Lothrop Company, 1888), p. 31. Much of this material is copied from the letter Anne wrote to G. W. Greene on March 17, 1879. She shared Henry's youthful years as Samuel did not. Fanny

Longfellow described visiting his family in 1843: sitting "up late. Talked with mother [ZWL] of Henry's early traits—his horror of guns, like mine, etc." Edward Wagenknecht, ed., *Mrs. Longfellow: Selected Letters and Journals of Fanny Appleton Longfellow, 1817-1861* (New York: Longmans, Green and Co., 1956), p. 90.

22. Newton Arvin, *Longfellow: His Life and Work* (Boston: Little, Brown and Company, 1962), p. 186. Letter, Samuel Longfellow to ALP, April 15, 1852, LNHS.

23. Harriet Lewis Bradley, "An Old House," *Remembrance Book*, pp. 99-100.

24. Samuel Longfellow "Longfellow's Boyhood," *Remembrance Book*, pp. 37-41.

25. McClatchy, *Poems*, pp. 340-342.

26. Letter, ALP to Elizabeth Orr, February 26, 1837, LNHS.

27. Hilen, *Letters*, 3:209. Letter, ZWL to MLG, December 12, 1850, LNHS.

28. Samuel Longfellow, ed., *Life of Henry Wadsworth Longfellow*, three volumes (Boston: Ticknor and Company, 1886-1887), 2:204.

29. Letter, ALP to MLG, November 11, 1849, LNHS.

30. Letter, ALP to MLG, March 14, 1851, LNHS.

31. Letter, ALP to Samuel Longfellow, February 25, 1851, LNHS.

32. Letter, ALP to MLG, April 13, 1850, LNHS.

33. Letters, ALP to MLG, 1851, and John Wadsworth to ALP, July 23, [1854], LNHS.

34. He sent $100 on a regular basis and in his will directed that Anne be given $500 annually. Hilen, *Letters*, 3:471; 6:805.

35. Cumberland County Registry of Deeds (January 26, 1901), Book 697, p. 343.

36. Letter, ALP to Samuel Longfellow, November 17, 1851, LNHS. William Sumner Appleton, Henry Longfellow's nephew, founded the Society for the Preservation of New England Antiquities in 1910. Alexander Wadsworth Longfellow, Jr., another nephew, became a leading colonial-revival architect in Boston, taking inspiration from New England's earliest houses.

37. Letters, ALP to James Greenleaf, December 2-4, 1843; ALP to MLG, March 27, 1853; ALP to Samuel Longfellow, April 25, 1853, LNHS. Alexander W. Longfellow, Jr., used "Old Original" to describe his photographs of the house, see his Scrapbook, ca. 1887, LNHS.

38. Letters, ALP to MLG, May 28, 1853, and April 21, 1864, LNHS. Alice Longfellow, the poet's daughter, a Vice Regent of the Mount Vernon Ladies' Association, helped arrange the furniture in the new house museum. *Portland Sunday Times*, July 21, 1901.

39. [Arthur Gerrier], *Wadsworth-Longfellow House: Historic Structure Report* (hereafter *HSR*), (Portsmouth, N.H.: Adams and Roy Consultants, Inc., 1987), p. 14.

40. *HSR*, pp. 18-19.

41. Letter, ZWL to Alexander W. Longfellow, May 16, 1836, LNHS. See Richard M. Candee, "'The Appearance of Enterprise and Improvement': Architecture and the Coastal Elite of Southern, Maine," in Sprague, *Agreeable Situations*, p. 72, and Portland tax assessments, 1800-1832, Collection 257, MHS.

42. *HSR*, pp. 28-29; letters, Peleg Wadsworth to George Wadsworth, September 24, 1814, Wadsworth Papers, MHS, and SL to ZWL, August 15, 1815, LNHS.

43. *HSR*, pp. 38, 40. Sprague, *Agreeable Situations*, cat. 68. SL paid Charles Elwell in 1831 for "setting a stove." See *HSR*, p. 41. *The Portland Advertiser* reported "Almost a fire" at the Longfellow House on March 12, 1862, in a second-floor chamber "from a stove funnel" running into the chamber above. Earle G. Shettleworth, Jr., kindly brought this reference to the author's attention. During an examination of the kitchen chimney in 2000, restoration mason Richard Irons observed evidence of another funnel leading from the kitchen through the hearth of the kitchen chamber, perhaps to access the flue in that room's chimney. A floor grate installed in the kitchen chamber ceiling helped warm the third floor.

44. *HSR*, p. 42.

45. Letter, ALP to Mary L. Greenleaf, April 21, 1864, LNHS. The circa 1890 cyanotypes by Mary King Longfellow are at LNHS. The privy permit has long been referenced, but it could not be confirmed by available city records.

46. For the documentation, see individual rooms in *HSR* and Laura Fecych Sprague, "Report of the Centennial Restoration," an addendum to the *HSR*, 2002.

47. See November 1867 photograph, LNHS. See also *List of*

ut Names Most Often Mentioned in the Poems of Henry *worth Longfellow and the Planting Plan and List of* *,ants in the Longfellow Garden* (Portland, Me.: Longfellow Garden Club, 1927).

48. Letter, ALP to Mary L. Greenleaf, November 11, 1851, LNHS.

49. A. J. Downing, *The Architecture of Country Houses* (1850 reprint, New York: Dover Publications, 1969), p. 369. Richard C. Nylander, Elizabeth Redmond, and Penny J. Sander, *Wallpaper in New England: Selections from the Society for the Preservation of New England Antiquities* (Boston: Mass.: Society for the Preservation of New England Antiquities, 1986), pp. 172-173. For the earlier choices, see Sprague, *Agreeable Situations*, cats. 67 & 68.

50. Letters, ZWL to SL, September 22, 1841; ALP to MLG, June 1852, LNHS.

51. Copy of "Aunt Anne's List, No. 3" [circa 1894], ex-collection Anne Longfellow Thorp, MHS, gift of Mrs. Bradford Wetherell, 2001. *Remembrance Book*, p. 89. After the death of Stephen Longfellow in 1849, one of the lolling chairs was given to Henry. It was returned to the Portland house by his daughter.

52. Downing, *Country Houses*, pp. 403-404.

53. Stephen Longfellow, insurance policies, November 17, 1825, MHS; Hilen, *Letters*, 1:305. A painted canvas floorcloth, which may have also carpeted the office, survives in the room's northeast closet. Nylander et al, *Wallpaper in New England*, pp. 198-199. Variations of the room's diaper paper survive in the George Creamer wallpaper sample book, nos. 1549 & 1611, Peabody Essex Museum.

54. *HSR*, pp. 53-57; Sprague, *Agreeable Situations*, p. 116 and cat. 49; Catalogue for sale of the law library of Stephen Longfellow, 1849, MHS.

55. Letter, ALP to MLG, March 27, 1853, LNHS.

56. Downing, *Country Houses*, p. 367.

57. Mary King Longfellow, "Aunt Anne under her own portrait, 1834-1897," Talbot photograph album, 1897-1898, Courtesy, the Talbot family. Sprague, *Agreeable Situations*, cats. 45, 79 and 138; letter, ALP to ZWL, July 9, 1840, LNHS. *Remembrance Book*, pp. 93-94.

58. Letter, ALP to MLG, April 1853, LNHS; Nylander et al, *Wallpaper in New England*, pp. 136, 182; Sprague, *Agreeable Situations*, cat. 130.

59. For Richard Irons's observations, see Sprague, "Report of the Centennial Restoration," 2002. Nathan Goold, *The Wadsworth-Longfellow House* (Portland, Me.: The Anthoensen Press, 1908), p. 38. Letters, ALP to MLG, October 28, 1850, and December 11, 1851, LNHS. Letter, ALP to HWL, January 5, 1853, Longfellow Papers, Houghton Library, Harvard University. Mary King Longfellow photographs, LNHS.

60. Brian Powell, *Wadsworth-Longfellow House: Interior Paint Study* (Dedham, Mass.: Building Conservation Associates, 2000), pp. 13-17; letters, ALP to MLG, April 24, 1853; and to Samuel Longfellow, April 25, 1853, LNHS. Downing, *Country Houses*, p. 370.

61. *HSR*, p. 33. Letter, ALP to MLG, June 15, 1852, LNHS; Alexander W. Longfellow, plan of porch and woodhouse, ca. 1850, LNHS. Richard Cohen kindly brought this drawing to the author's attention.

62. Sprague, *Agreeable Situations*, cat. 50; The table is illustrated in *Remembrance Book*, p. [99]. Thomas Hardiman, Jr., "Veneered Furniture of Cumston and Buckminster, Saco, Maine," *The Magazine Antiques*, vol. 159, no. 5 (May 2001): 754-761. *HSR*, p. 81.

63. *HSR*, p. 76.

64. Bangs, *Historic Mansion*, p. 707.

65. Copy of "Aunt Anne's List, No. 2" [1890], ex-collection Anne Longfellow Thorp, MHS, gift of Mrs. Bradford Wetherell, 2001.

66. Letter, SL to ZWL, August 15, 1815, LNHS.

67. From *The Golden Mile-Stone* (1854) in *The Poetical Works of Longfellow* (Boston: Houghton Mifflin Co., 1975), pp. 195-196.